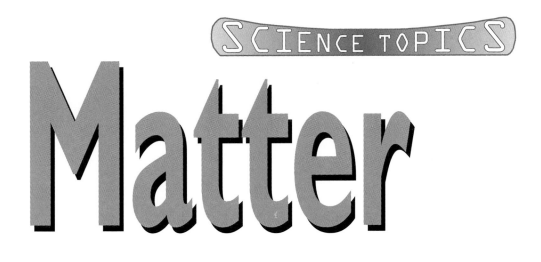

Matter

ANN FULLICK

Heinemann Library
Des Plaines, Illinois

Designed by AMR
Illustrations by Art Construction
Printed in Hong Kong

03 02 01 00 99
10 9 8 7 6 5 4 3 2 1

Fullick, Ann, 1956-
    Matter / Ann Fullick.
        p.   cm. -- (Science topics)
    Includes bibliographical references and index.
    Summary: Discusses various aspects of matter, including atoms,
molecules, elements, compounds, states of matter, expanding and
contracting, and other physical and chemical changes.
    ISBN 1-57572-767-6 (library binding)
    1. Matter--Constitution--Juvenile literature. 2. Matter-
-Properties--Juvenile literature. [1. Matter.] I. Title.
II. Series.
QC173.16.F85   1998
530.4--dc21   98-11589
                                                        CIP
                                                        AC

Acknowledgments
The Publishers would like to thank the following for permission to reproduce photographs:
Ann Ronan at Image Select/The Nobel Foundation pg. 4; Anthony Blake Photo Library/Tony
Robins pg. 10; Bass Museum pg. 15; G.S.F. Picture Library pg. 8; Image Select/NASA pg. 18,
/C.F.C.L. pg. 25; Milepost $92\frac{1}{2}$ pg. 14; Pix S.A. pgs. 9, 11, 22, 29; Science Photo Library/Alfred
Pasieka pg. 19, /John Sanford pg. 21; Tony Stone Images/Paul Wakefield pg. 12; Telegraph Color
Library/Carl Roessler pg. 17.

Cover photograph reproduced with permission of Science Photo Library/Secchi Lecaque/
Roussel-Uclaf/CNRI. Cover shows a human cell over a background image of an atom.

Our thanks to Kris Stutchbury for her help in the preparation of this edition.

Every effort has been made to contact copyright holders of any material reproduced in this
book. Any omissions will be rectified in subsequent printings if notice is given to the Publisher.

Any words appearing in the text in bold, **like this**, are explained in the Glossary.

Contents

Atoms and Molecules

Everything around us—**solids**, **liquids**, and **gases**—is made of matter. But what is matter made of? The accepted idea at the moment is that everything around us is made up of **particles** which are too small to see, even with the most powerful microscope.

SCIENCE ESSENTIALS

All substances are made up of particles called **atoms**. Atoms often join together to form **molecules**. Different substances are made up of different molecules.

Models of matter

Atoms make up everything around us—living and non-living. Atoms are so small no one has yet seen them, even with the most advanced, modern technology. All we can do is observe the ways in which matter behaves, and try to explain what we see. Over the centuries scientists have developed **models** of matter to explain how materials work—for example, to explain why solids keep their shape and why some substances react together when others do not. As research has provided new bits of information, the models have gradually changed.

The scientist Neils Bohr (right) developed this early model of the structure of an atom (below) dating from 1913. In the last 150 years, scientists have been developing an understanding of the complex models of matter.

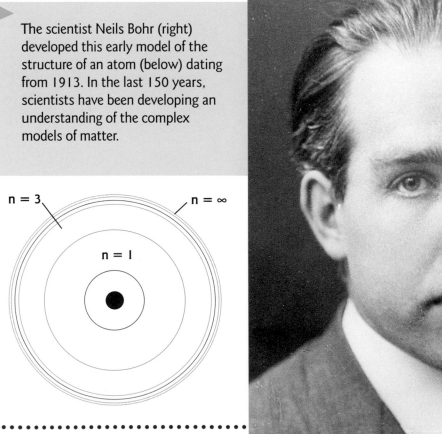

$n = 3$

$n = \infty$

$n = 1$

Atoms and molecules

Matter is made of particles—this model is the best one we have to explain the way materials behave. But the particles themselves are not the same in every material. Most materials are made up of particles called molecules. These molecules are characteristic of the particular material. For example, all water molecules look the same, and they all look different from any other molecule. A water molecule is the smallest particle of water you can get.

Molecules themselves are made up of combinations of even smaller particles known as atoms. Atoms are the basic units of all materials. Some molecules are quite simple, made up of two or three atoms joined together. Other molecules are much more complicated and are made up of hundreds or thousands of individual atoms.

Sugar is made up of molecules of sucrose. Each molecule contains atoms of carbon, hydrogen, and oxygen joined together in a unique arrangement.

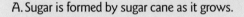

A. Sugar is formed by sugar cane as it grows.

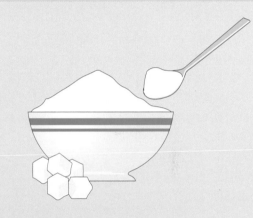

B. The sugar is purified and produced in crystals for use in food manufacture and in cooking.

C. The sugar crystals are made up of sugar molecules. Their chemical name is sucrose.

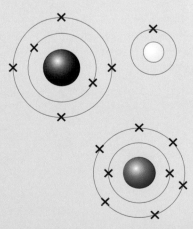

D. The sucrose molecules are made up of atoms of carbon (C), hydrogen (H), and oxygen (O).

Elements and Compounds

All substances are made up of **atoms**. A substance made up from only one type of atom is an element. There are 91 **elements** that occur naturally on Earth. These elements can combine to make an almost infinite number of **compounds**.

SCIENCE ESSENTIALS

If elements combine chemically, they form compounds. These compounds have new and often quite different properties from the original elements.

Elements

Scientific ideas about elements were borrowed from Greek philosophers who lived more than 2,000 years ago. They believed that everything was made up from four basic substances or "elements"—air, earth, fire, and water—and that combinations of these four elements in different proportions gave other substances their observable properties. Our ideas have changed since those times. We now say that an element is a substance made up of one type of atom. There are 107 elements that have been discovered. Only 91 of them are found naturally. The others have only been called into brief existence in laboratories. Most of the elements are **solids** at room temperature, although 10 are **gases** and 2 are **liquids**. We are totally unaware of many of these elements, as they only appear in our lives as parts of **molecules** in complex materials. Others—such as the carbon in our pencils—are found in common objects that are used daily. The oxygen we take into our bodies every time we breathe is vital for our survival.

Chlorine is a greenish-yellow, poisonous gas that is very important in many compounds. For years it has been used in very small amounts, **dissolved** in water, to keep swimming pools clean.

Carbon is an element that is found in the soft graphite used in pencil "leads" and in the incredibly hard and expensive diamond.

Chlorine and carbon are examples of **non-metal** elements.

Most metals are not found as elements—they are found combined with other chemicals in rocks known as ores.

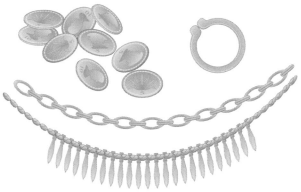

But gold, although rare, is found in its pure state. People have valued it and used it for coins and jewelry for thousands of years.

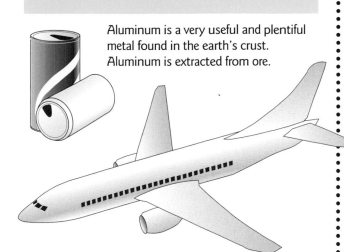

Gold and aluminum are two **metal** elements.

Aluminum is a very useful and plentiful metal found in the earth's crust. Aluminum is extracted from ore.

Elements from above?

Iron is a metal not usually found in its pure form on Earth. But some of the meteorites that crash through the earth's atmosphere from outer space are almost pure iron. The giant meteorite, which many believe brought about the end of the dinosaurs, may have been an enormous lump of iron several miles across. Our ancestors collected and prized this "metal from heaven." Today we value such meteorites as a fascinating source of information about the universe beyond our own planet.

Compounds

Elements are pure substances—they can not be split into anything smaller. Chop up a nugget of gold and you will simply get smaller and smaller pieces of gold until you are down to atoms of gold.

When a compound is formed, the atoms of one element collide with the atoms of another element and join together in a **chemical reaction**. Well-known examples of compounds are salt, NaCl (sodium and chlorine joined together); and nitric acid, HNO_3 (hydrogen, nitrogen, and oxygen joined together).

If you split water into smaller and smaller droplets, you would reach the individual molecules of water. You could then split these into the individual atoms of oxygen and hydrogen, the elements that originally joined together to form the water.

Compounds and Mixtures

The world in which we live is a complex combination of **mixtures** and **compounds**. How can we distinguish between them?

Mixtures matter

Mixtures are an important part of planet Earth. About two-thirds of the earth's surface is covered by seas—and sea water is a mixture of salt and water along with a few other mineral salts. Take a deep breath of air—you are pulling a mixture of **gases** into your lungs. Once there, your body quickly separates the oxygen that you need from the other gases in the air. Even the crust of the earth is made up of a mixture of different materials— but many of those materials are compounds. What is the difference between mixtures and compounds?

A mixture contains two or more separate substances that are mixed together physically but do not combine chemically, such as a mixture of sand and salt, or salt and water. Compounds are formed when there is a **chemical reaction** between two or more elements. The different types of **atoms** become joined together, and they cannot be separated by physical processes such as heating or cooling, **distillation**, using magnets, or **filtering**. Chemical reactions can be shown in the form of word equations like these:

hydrogen + oxygen → water
sodium + chlorine → sodium chloride

When salt and water are mixed, the salt **dissolves** in the water, but the two can easily be separated again if the water **evaporates** away leaving crystals of salt.

Making compounds

When **elements** combine during a chemical reaction to form compounds, an energy change is involved. This may mean that energy is taken in or given out, but once the energy change has taken place, the reaction cannot be reversed. In many reactions the energy change is hard to see, but in some it is very clear!

Reactions where energy is taken in are relatively rare. When they happen you can feel the temperature drop if you are holding the test-tube as the reaction takes place. More often energy is given out, with heat and sometimes light produced as a reaction progresses.

▶ The chemicals needed to produce spectacular displays like this are mixed together and stored in the firework. Only when there is an input of energy (lighting the touch paper) does a chemical reaction take place, forming new compounds and releasing lots of light, heat, and sound in the process.

Some of the **gases** in the mixture that make up our air are elements (oxygen and nitrogen), but others are compounds (carbon dioxide, water). Sea water is also a mixture of compounds—sodium chloride (salt) and water. Both compounds and mixtures play vital roles in the structure of the earth . . . and in our lives.

SCIENCE ESSENTIALS

When elements are mixed together, they keep their individual properties and can be relatively easily separated.
When elements combine chemically to form compounds, they have new and different properties and cannot be separated except by further chemical reactions.

Separating Mixtures

The clearest difference between a **mixture** and a **compound** is that the components of a mixture can be separated from each other in a number of ways.

Filtering things

One of the simplest ways of separating a mixture is to use filtration. This is a principle used in everyday life. When we make a cup of tea, we use a mixture of tea leaves and water. We actually want to drink the water flavored by the tea leaves, but not the leaves themselves. So, by one means or another we filter it.

Similar principles are used in science all of the time. If we have a mixture of two **solids**, and one of them can be **dissolved** in water and one cannot, then an easy way to separate them is to put the mixture in water. One of the solids dissolves, and the other does not.

One solid can then be obtained by filtering as a solid residue. The other can be obtained from the filtered liquid by heating gently to **evaporate** the water. Water is a **solvent** that is used frequently, but techniques like this also work with other solvents, such as **methylated spirits.**

Whether we pour the tea through a tea strainer or simply use a tea bag, we are separating the liquid part of the tea that we want from the solid part of the mixture that we don't want.

Chromatography

Chromatography is used to separate mixtures of colored substances, such as inks and dyes.

The different dyes travel at different speeds across a filter paper. As a result, the colors separate and can be seen.

Genetic fingerprinting

Special kinds of chromatography have been developed using specific gels and electricity. These can be used with substances that are not colored.

One of the most exciting uses of these techniques has been the ability to separate out and identify human **DNA**, the genetic material that makes each of us unique. By analyzing the DNA from human tissue in this way, criminals who might have gotten away with their crimes have been convicted. In other cases, some innocent people have been set free. **Genetic fingerprinting** is a powerful piece of chemical analysis!

Distillation

Distillation in the laboratory involves heating a mixture of **liquids** until the **boiling** point of one of them is reached. At this point, the liquid changes state and becomes a **gas**, which is then collected and cooled.

Distillation relies on the fact that different substances have different boiling points. A mixture containing two liquids can be completely separated by this method. If there are more than two liquids, once the first has boiled off, heating can continue until the boiling point of a second liquid is reached. Separating liquids like this is known as **fractional distillation**.

When crude oil comes out of the ground, it is a brownish-black, odorous, thick liquid that would be no good as a fuel for anything. But the main part of the process of refining oil to make it ready for use involves fractional distillation. The crude oil is heated to relatively high temperatures. As the gas cools down, different fractions are collected. For example, gasoline **condenses** between 68°F (20°C) and 158°F (70°C). Its main use is as fuel in cars. Gas oil condenses at 482°F to 662°F (250°C to 350°C) and is used to make diesel fuel and central heating oil.

Within an oil refinery's maze of towers and piping, black crude oil is split into a range of useful fractions.

States of Matter

Everything on Earth is in one of three states—**solid**, **liquid**, or **gas.** The properties of these states can be explained by looking at what is happening to the **particles** making up the materials.

SCIENCE ESSENTIALS
The **particles** in **solids, liquids,** and **gases** are always moving at room temperature.

States of matter

We probably all know what to expect from a solid, a liquid, and a gas. But how do we quantify the differences in a scientific way?

Solids keep their shape and volume. They do not flow to take up the shape of any container they are put in, they are relatively dense, and they are not easily compressed (squashed).

Liquids, on the other hand, do not maintain their shape—but they do maintain their volume. They flow and take on the shape of any container into which they are poured. Generally they are less dense than solids, but like solids they are not easily compressed.

Gases maintain neither their shape nor their volume—they will fill any container, however large or small. They flow freely, have a very low density, and are readily compressed.

Most materials can exist in any of these states. We are familiar with ice, water, and steam in our everyday lives. Most other substances can also appear as solids, liquids, and gases. How can we explain this ability of single substances to appear in such different states?

In this picture, there are three states of matter—the ice is solid water, there is liquid water, too, and the air surrounding them is made up of a number of different gases.

Moving models

The particles in matter are constantly moving, although as the temperature gets lower the movement slows. The only time movement stops is at 0°K (–459°F or –273°C). This is known as **absolute zero**—the lowest temperature possible. At that temperature all particle movement in every known type of matter comes to a stop.

The easiest way to understand the properties of solids, liquids, and gases is to imagine what is happening to the particles they are made of.

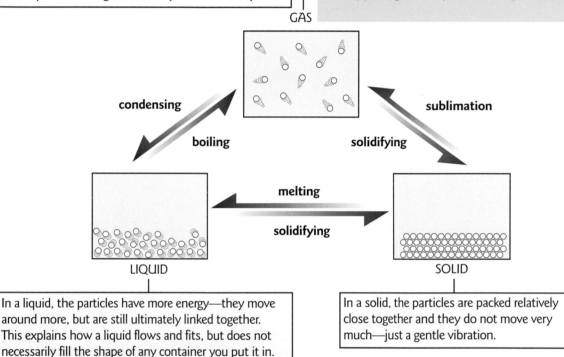

In a gas, the particles are moving with so much energy that they break free of one another and move anywhere. This explains how a gas will fill any container it is put in.

GAS

condensing

sublimation

boiling

solidifying

melting

solidifying

LIQUID

SOLID

In a liquid, the particles have more energy—they move around more, but are still ultimately linked together. This explains how a liquid flows and fits, but does not necessarily fill the shape of any container you put it in.

In a solid, the particles are packed relatively close together and they do not move very much—just a gentle vibration.

Solids as liquids

Some substances we think of as solids are really super-cooled liquids. The most common example of this is glass. Every glass window you see is really a sheet of incredibly thick liquid that is flowing infinitely slowly down the pane. Glass that is several hundred years old is measurably thicker at the bottom than at the top. But at other times real solids act as if they were liquids—providing us with a visible **model** for how a liquid works. Huge masses of grain flowing into silos move and flow like a liquid. Perhaps the most treacherous of all examples is when the earth beneath our feet acts like a liquid—during earthquakes and in quicksands—and people drown in soil or sand that no longer supports their weight, but flows around them.

Expanding and Contracting

In the world around us, materials are constantly getting bigger and shrinking again in response to changes in temperature.

Hotter bigger, colder smaller?

When many materials are heated, they **expand** (get bigger). The expansion may not be much—usually too small to be noticed with the naked eye—but it can affect us in many ways. Materials expand because the **particles** that they are made of absorb energy as they are heated. As a result, they move more. To move more, they need more space, so they force each other slightly further apart. This causes the material to expand. Most materials contract (get smaller) when the temperature drops. This is because the particles making up the material have less energy, and so they move less. If they are moving less, they take up less space and so keep closer together. This causes the material to **contract**.

How does it affect us?

Some of the effects of expansion and contraction are quite trivial. If you put the top on a bottle or jar tightly and then put it in the refrigerator to store it, it may be almost impossible to open when you go to use it again. This is because as the lid gets cold, it contracts to fit even more tightly. Fortunately, in this situation there is a simple solution—running the top under warm water will cause it to expand again and loosen.

Metals are particularly prone to expansion. Railway lines have to be laid with gaps between the rails so that when the rails expand in the summer heat they do not push against each other. If they do, the forces that result from the expansion of the metal are sufficient to buckle the rails.

Concrete paving slabs must have gaps between them to allow for expansion, and roads made out of concrete sections have spaces filled with rubbery mastic between them. If the blocks were laid without gaps, the forces from expansion in the summer heat could crack the concrete.

We use the expansion and contraction of materials to make certain processes possible, particularly when we need a piece of metal to fit tightly over something else. The metal piece is heated strongly and put in place when it is hot and expanded. When it cools down and contracts, it will be held very firmly in place. Putting the metal tires on train wheels and, more traditionally, the metal hoops on wooden barrels, all depend on the expansion and contraction of metal.

It is not just **solids** that expand when they are heated. Liquids and **gases** do the same. Many of the thermometers we use to measure temperature depend on the fact that the mercury or ethanol in them expands as the temperature goes up and contracts as the temperature falls. This gives a rise or fall in the level of liquid in the tube and thus a different temperature reading.

For centuries, coopers (barrel makers) have used the expansion and contraction of metals to fit the metal hoops around barrels.

Teething troubles?

When we use two materials together, it is important that they expand and contract at similar rates in response to a change in temperature. Reinforced concrete is an invaluable building material. Steel is used for the rods that strengthen the concrete because steel and concrete both expand by the same amount for a 50°F (10°C) rise in temperature. If they expanded at different rates, the concrete would be fractured by the stresses set up. When dentists fill a tooth, they have the same problem—if the filling material does not expand and contract at the same rate as the tooth itself, patients would end up with fractured teeth after a cup of hot tea or a cold ice cream cone!

Gas On the Go!

In **gases**, the **particles** are moving around fast and freely. This explains many of their properties.

Gas pressure

As gas particles move about rapidly, they collide with other particles and with the sides of the container they are in. The collisions with the side of the container cause the gas to exert a pressure. The more frequent the collisions, the greater the pressure. **Gas pressure** gives a measure of the number and frequency of these collisions.

The pressure of a gas is affected by the volume of the container the gas is in and by the temperature of the gas. If the temperature stays the same, increasing the volume of the container will lower the pressure of a given amount of gas. This is because the particles have to travel further before they meet the walls, and so are less likely to collide with them.

Similarly, if the temperature stays the same, decreasing the volume of the container will increase the pressure of the gas inside it.

Diffusion

People buy perfume and aftershave because they want to smell nice, but without **diffusion** they would be wasting their money. As air **molecules** move about rapidly in all directions other particles also get involved. Molecules of the perfume or aftershave you put on your skin move and mix with the air molecules around them. They are then carried large distances as a result of all the random high-speed movement that is going on. This is how they reach the sensory cells in other people's noses.

Diffusion also occurs in **liquids**, although as the particles are moving less quickly, the process takes longer.

Gases also diffuse into liquids—when the gas particles hit the surface of the liquid, they sometimes go in and mix with the liquid particles. This is how oxygen from the air becomes **dissolved** in water, which is vital for all water-living animals, such as fish.

SCIENCE ESSENTIALS

Gas **particles** move at high speeds and collide with anything that gets in their way. The collisions result in a measurable gas pressure. The movement of the gas particles means that they rapidly mix together—this is known as **diffusion.**

Divers beware!

Divers who maintain the pipework of oil rigs or conduct research in the sea need to work at great depths under water for long periods of time. To avoid repeated periods of **decompression,** they live in special chambers for days at a time.

When gas is under pressure, more of it will dissolve in a liquid. So when divers go deep underwater to explore or work, more of the gases they breathe dissolve in their blood than normal.

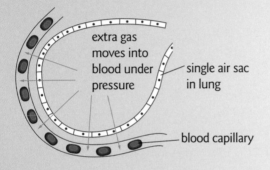

extra gas moves into blood under pressure

single air sac in lung

blood capillary

To prevent "the bends," divers have to return to the surface very slowly over a period of hours, allowing the body to adjust at stages along the way—this is known as decompression.

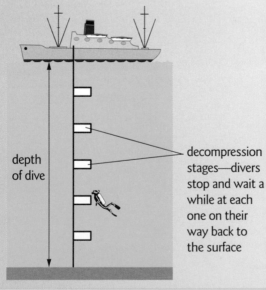

depth of dive

decompression stages—divers stop and wait a while at each one on their way back to the surface

These chambers are maintained at the pressure the divers are working at, so they do not need to decompress before coming in for a meal and a rest. They simply undergo a single slow decompression at the end of their shift. Working like this is known as **saturation diving**.

The dissolved gases are not a problem while the divers remain deep underwater. However, if divers return to the surface too quickly, the gas diffuses back out of their blood as tiny bubbles in their blood vessels or joints. This can cause agonizing pain known as "the bends."

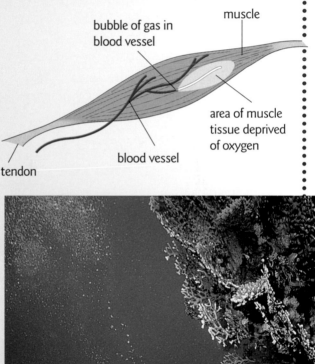

muscle

bubble of gas in blood vessel

area of muscle tissue deprived of oxygen

blood vessel

tendon

▶ The diffusion of gases into liquids can cause problems for divers working deep under the sea. However, most divers can enjoy the beauty of the ocean without the need for major decompression.

Dissolving

When people add sugar to their tea or coffee, the crystals disappear and the drink becomes sweet-tasting—the sugar has **dissolved**.

How do things dissolve?

The fact that the model of matter is made up of moving **particles** helps us to understand what happens when a solid, like salt, **dissolves** in a **liquid**, like water. The particles of solid salt placed in the water are vibrating, but they are held together by the **elastic forces** between them. In the water, the particles are moving about more freely, and some collide with salt particles on the outside of the salt crystal.

If these collisions take place with enough force, some of the salt particles are loosened from the solid structure. Once loose, they spread through the water by **diffusion** as a result of random movement and collisions of the particles in the liquid. This in turn means more salt particles are exposed on the outside of the crystal, and gradually the whole thing dissolves.

We can speed up the rate at which solids dissolve by increasing the area of solid particles exposed to the liquid or by increasing the speed at which the liquid particles are moving. The main ways of speeding up the process are heating the liquid, stirring or shaking the mixture, or crushing the **solute** before mixing it with the **solvent**. A point will be reached after which no more solute will dissolve— this is called a **saturated solution**.

▶ Two-thirds of the earth's surface is covered by oceans which are a solution of solid salt crystals (a solute) in water (a solvent).

Water—the wonder-solvent

Water is probably the single most important solvent we know. Many different chemicals dissolve in water. Once substances are dissolved in water, they can react together much more easily.

The **chemical reactions** that make up living organisms all take place in solution in water. An enormous range of reactions in the chemical, drug, and food industries are also based on chemicals dissolving in water.

However, not everything dissolves in water. Substances that do not—oil, chalk, sand—are called **insoluble**.

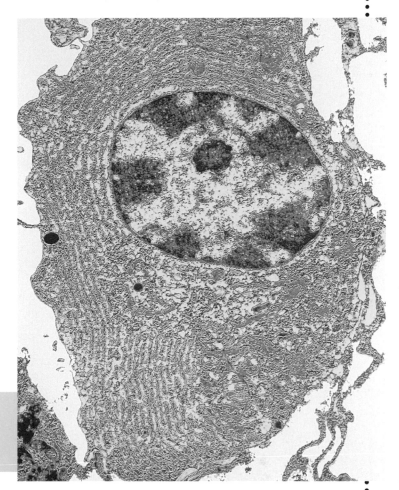

All the chemical reactions that occur in a human cell like this one, or any other living cell, take place in solution in water.

*S*tick with it!

Almost any liquid can act as a solvent. Some of the most frequently used (after water) are organic solvents, such as ethanol and tetrachloromethane. These will dissolve solids insoluble in water. They are of great importance in the production of adhesives, which are useful for sticking all sorts of things together. Some of these solvents **evaporate** very quickly when exposed to air. This is useful if you want the adhesive to dry quickly. This is becoming increasingly important as adhesives are used to replace other ways of joining materials together. The use of these organic solvents in adhesives does carry some risks, however. Some of the solvents create an artificial "high" if they are breathed in, and this has led to solvent abuse and the deaths of a number of young people. And in cases where the solvent dries very fast and the adhesive is very powerful (as in "superglues") a number of people have found themselves stuck either to other parts of their own body or to an object they were trying to fix!

Changing State

Matter not only exists in different states, it regularly changes state in response to changes in temperature or pressure. These changes are physical and can easily be reversed.

Elastic "bonds"

The **particles** in **solids** and **liquids** are held together by **elastic forces** that allow the particles to move but keeps them fairly close together. Energy is always involved when matter changes state, because it takes energy to make or break these **forces.**

SCIENCE ESSENTIALS

In a **solid** substance, the **particles** are held close together by **elastic forces** between them.
Heating causes some of the forces holding the solid particles together to break so it **melts**, becoming a **liquid**.
Further heating causes the liquid to **boil**, breaking all the forces and turning it into a **gas**.
The total **mass** of the substance stays the same during all of these **physical changes**.

Getting hotter

When a solid is heated, enough energy may be transfered to some of the particles for them to break free of the forces holding them close to other particles. If this happens, the solid **melts** to form a liquid. However, sufficient forces remain in place to maintain the volume of the liquid. If the heating continues, enough energy may be transfered to all of the particles for them to break free of each other and move around rapidly in all directions as they become a **gas.** At this point, the liquid is **boiling** and the volume increases enormously unless the gas is kept under great pressure.

Different materials change state at different temperatures. Some are only liquids (L) and solids (S) close to **absolute zero**, while others only become gases (G) at very high temperatures.

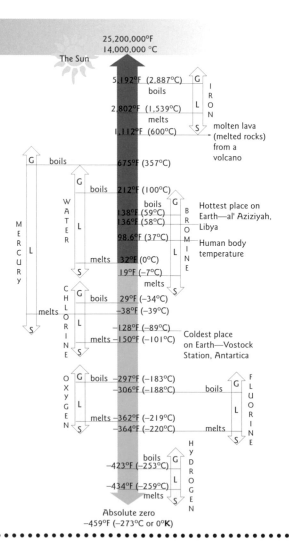

25,200,000°F
14,000,000 °C
The Sun

5,192°F (2,887°C) boils — IRON
2,802°F (1,539°C) melts — IRON
1,112°F (600°C) — molten lava (melted rocks) from a volcano

675°F (357°C)

212°F (100°C) boils — WATER
138°F (59°C) boils — BROMINE
136°F (58°C)
98.6°F (37°C) — Hottest place on Earth—al' Aziziyah, Libya
— Human body temperature
32°F (0°C) melts — WATER
19°F (−7°C) melts — BROMINE

29°F (−34°C) boils — CHLORINE
−38°F (−39°C) — MERCURY

−128°F (−89°C)
−150°F (−101°C) melts — CHLORINE — Coldest place on Earth—Vostock Station, Antartica

−297°F (−183°C) boils — OXYGEN
−306°F (−188°C) boils — FLUORINE
−362°F (−219°C) melts — OXYGEN
−364°F (−220°C) melts — FLUORINE

−423°F (−253°C) boils — HYDROGEN
−434°F (−259°C) melts — HYDROGEN

Absolute zero
−459°F (−273°C or 0°K)

Getting colder

When matter cools, the particles get closer to each other again and energy is transferred out of the system. The forces between the particles form again, and, as they do, the substance changes from a gas to a liquid (**condenses**) and finally **solidifies** back to a solid again.

Changes in state are physical changes—the particles stay the same, but they are arranged in a different way. There are the same number of particles involved in all the different states.

The total mass of the substance stays the same as it changes from solid to liquid to gas and back again. Most substances expand as they get hotter and contract as they cool down again. Water is an interesting exception—it expands as it cools down from 39°F (4°C) to 32°F (0°C), when it solidifies to form ice. This is why ice (32°F or 0°C) floats on water, trapping a layer of warmer(39°F or 4°C) water beneath it, and many living things survive the winter in warmer water under the ice.

Star states

Not every material can exist in every state. For example, wood reacts with the oxygen in the air and burns long before it reaches a temperature at which it might melt, so it never reaches a liquid or gaseous state.

More intriguing still are the stars in the sky, which scientists think represent a fourth state of matter. This state, known as **plasma**, does not exist naturally on Earth. Plasma results from a breakdown in the structure of the **atoms** themselves, existing as a "soup" of **sub-atomic** particles.

▶ The very atoms that make up all matter are themselves made up of even smaller (sub-atomic) particles. The stars we see in the night sky are made up of these particles freed from the atoms that contained them.

Physical and Chemical Changes

After crude oil has been **distilled**, it is possible to mix all of the products together and get back to the original black, smelly **liquid**. On the other hand, when some of the products of crude oil are reacted together to produce plastics, the process cannot be reversed. What is the difference?

Physical changes

Physical changes include changing state—**dissolving**, **evaporating**, and **condensing**—and are reversible. When we write word or chemical equations for changes of state, it is therefore really important to show the state of the substances involved. For example:

water (s) + heat → water (l) + heat → water (g)
ice (solid)   water (liquid)   steam (gas)

SCIENCE ESSENTIALS

During **physical** and **chemical changes,** mass is conserved. In other words, there is the same **mass** of material at the end of the reactions as there was at the beginning. This is because the number of **atoms** stays the same, even though they may be arranged in a different way.

▼

Physical reactions involve changes in the arrangement or movement of the **particles** making up matter. They do not involve any chemical interactions.

When matter changes state from liquid to **gas** (for example, water turning to steam when it boils in a kettle), the arrangement and level of movement of the particles changes, but the number and type of particles stays the same. This means that the state of change is easily reversed.

Processes such as **fractional distillation** (as used in the distillation of oil shown in the diagram to the right) involve physical changes that are easily reversed.

fractions collected

HEAT

gas enters

Melting materials such as metals, wax, or rocks, all involve changing the movement of the particles, but not changing the particles themselves. The changes are reversed when the source of heat is removed and the material, like this molten metal, cools down and **solidifies**.

Chemical reactions

Chemical reactions take place when atoms of different substances collide with enough energy to react and join together. Chemical reactions may take place between **elements**, an element and a **compound**, or two compounds. Sometimes, but not always, they will involve a change of state as well.

There are many different kinds of chemical reactions, but they all involve **atoms** or **molecules** of different substances joining together. Most **chemical changes** are one-way reactions—they can not easily be reversed.

For example, when the gray metal magnesium reacts with hydrochloric acid, bubbles of hydrogen gas are produced and a solution of magnesium chloride is formed. The particles of the **reactants** have rearranged themselves to form different products. The same metal—magnesium—will react with the colorless gas oxygen in the air to form the white powder magnesium oxide. Atoms of the two elements combine in a reaction that releases a great deal of light and heat energy, and the process is not easily reversed.

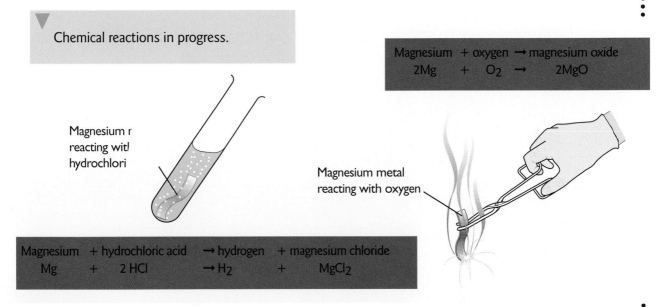

Chemical reactions in progress.

Magnesium r
reacting with
hydrochlori

Magnesium metal reacting with oxygen

Magnesium + oxygen → magnesium oxide
2Mg + O_2 → 2MgO

Magnesium + hydrochloric acid → hydrogen + magnesium chloride
Mg + 2 HCl → H_2 + $MgCl_2$

Chemical complexity

Not all chemical reactions are simple. For example, when living things eat food, an enormous variety of chemical reactions takes place. These reactions break down the huge food molecules containing thousands of atoms into small molecules. The small molecules can then be used in further chemical reactions to provide energy and to build up new large molecules to construct living cells.

Inside Atoms and Molecules

The way materials behave is largely a result of the arrangement of the **atoms** and **molecules** they are made of. By looking inside these atoms and **molecules**, we have a much better understanding of the way things behave, and also make predictions about what they might do next!

SCIENCE ESSENTIALS

Atoms have a **nucleus** containing **protons** and **neutrons** with **electrons** moving around it. The atoms of different **elements** contain different numbers of protons.

Inside an atom

There are 91 elements that occur naturally. Each atom of any particular element contains the same number of **protons** and **electrons.** Protons carry a positive charge and electrons carry a negative charge. As atoms are always neutral, the number of protons and electrons must always be the same so that they cancel each other out. Hence, the number of protons determines the number of electrons.

It is the arrangement of the electrons that determines how the atom will react with others. The arrangement of electrons in layers around the nucleus of the atom determines whether an element is very **reactive** or very unreactive, and the type of bonds it can form with other atoms.

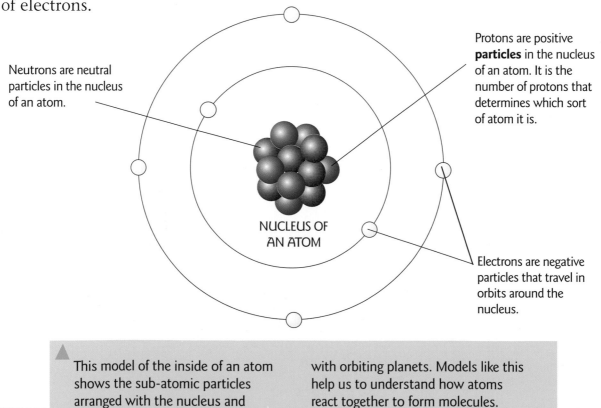

Neutrons are neutral particles in the nucleus of an atom.

Protons are positive **particles** in the nucleus of an atom. It is the number of protons that determines which sort of atom it is.

NUCLEUS OF AN ATOM

Electrons are negative particles that travel in orbits around the nucleus.

This model of the inside of an atom shows the sub-atomic particles arranged with the nucleus and electrons looking rather like a sun with orbiting planets. Models like this help us to understand how atoms react together to form molecules.

Atomic number

The **atomic number** of an element tells us how many protons are in the nucleus. Hydrogen has an atomic number of 1, carbon 6, and oxygen 8. Rather than write out the full name of elements all the time, we represent them with one or two letters. Some of these are obvious, such as H for hydrogen and O for oxygen. However, others are much more obscure—lead is Pb from the Latin *plumbus* which meant "lead." So by writing $_8O$ or $_{82}Pb$ we can tell other scientists quite a lot about the element we are dealing with.

Using isotopes

The number of neutrons sometimes varies even in atoms of the same element. Atoms of the same element that have the same atomic number but different numbers of neutrons are known as **isotopes**. The difference shows up in the **mass** of the atoms. Some isotopes are also **radioactive**. This makes them very useful to scientists and doctors because they can be used to keep track of substances in animal and plant systems, to follow what is happening inside the body, or to treat specific illnesses.

Making molecules

The 91 naturally occurring elements are the chemical alphabet. It is from combinations of the atoms of these elements that the molecules of all other chemical **compounds** are made. When atoms react together to form molecules, they may share their outer electrons with another atom, or they may give or receive electrons from another atom. Whichever way they join, there is only one combination of atoms that can make up a particular compound.

Just as the letters H-E-L-L-O always spell *Hello* and F-R-E-D spell *Fred*, water is always H_2O (two atoms of hydrogen joined to one of oxygen)

and methane is always CH_4 (four atoms of hydrogen joined to one of carbon). Chemical formulas tell us exactly how many atoms of which elements are joined together to make a very specific compound.

▶ The methane flare (CH_4) on this oil rig is burning with oxygen (O_2) to form carbon dioxide (CO_2) and water (H_2O).

$$CH_4 + 2O_2 \rightarrow CO_2 + 2H_2O$$

The Periodic Table

The **atomic number** of the **elements** indicates the number of **protons** (and therefore **electrons**) in their **atoms**. This in turn determines how easily they will react.

If we arrange the elements in order of their atomic number in a **Periodic Table**, clear patterns emerge in the way they behave. Some of these are explained below.

▼ The Periodic Table.

Group I elements are the most **reactive metals** on Earth and they get more reactive as you move down the group. Because they are very soft and highly reactive, they are rarely used in their pure form but they make very stable and useful compounds.

A street light uses sodium light.

Sports Drink

Contains
Sodium
Potassium

Group II elements are a group of slightly less reactive metals, although they react more easily as you move down the group. For example, radium is **radioactive**.

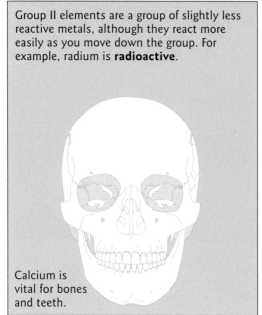

Calcium is vital for bones and teeth.

Group I	Group II									
lithium **Li** 3	**Be** 4									
sodium **Na** 11	magnesium **Mg** 12									
potassium **K** 19	calcium **Ca** 20	**Sc** 21	titanium **Ti** 22	**V** 23	chromium **Cr** 24	**Mn** 25	iron **Fe** 26	cobalt **Co** 27		
rubidium **Rb** 37	**Sr** 38	**Y** 39	**Zr** 40	**Nb** 41	**Mo** 42	**Tc** 43	**Ru** 44	**Rh** 45		
Cs 55	**Ba** 56	**La** 57	**Hf** 72	**Ta** 73	**W** 74	**Re** 75	**Os** 76	**Ir** 77		
Fr 87	radium **Ra** 88	**Ac** 89								

hydrogen **H** 1 — Hydrogen is on its own

17 other rare elements ending with

uranium **U** 92

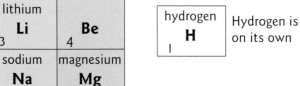

This big block of elements is known as the **transition elements**. They include some very strong, hard metals like iron and copper which people have used for many thousands of years.

The lines across the periodic table are known as **periods**. Across each period the elements change from **reactive** metals to **non-reactive non-metals**.

The lines down the periodic table are known as groups. The elements in each group usually have similar properties and may react more easily or less easily with other chemicals as you move down the group.

We can use these patterns to predict how different elements will react to each other or with a different **compound**.

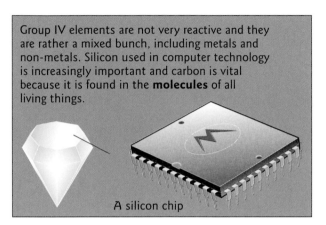

Group IV elements are not very reactive and they are rather a mixed bunch, including metals and non-metals. Silicon used in computer technology is increasingly important and carbon is vital because it is found in the **molecules** of all living things.

A silicon chip

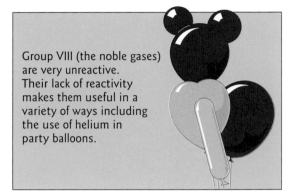

Group VIII (the noble gases) are very unreactive. Their lack of reactivity makes them useful in a variety of ways including the use of helium in party balloons.

			Group III	Group IV	Group V	Group VI	Group VII	Group VIII
								helium **He** 2
			B 5	carbon **C** 6	nitrogen **N** 7	oxygen **O** 8	fluorine **F** 9	neon **Ne** 10
			aluminum **Al** 13	silicon **Si** 14	phosphorus **P** 15	sulphur **S** 16	chlorine **Cl** 17	argon **Ar** 18
nickel **Ni** 28	copper **Cu** 29	zinc **Zn** 30	**Ga** 31	**Ge** 32	**As** 33	**Se** 34	bromine **Br** 35	**Kr** 36
Pd 46	silver **Ag** 47	**Cd** 48	**In** 49	tin **Sn** 50	**Sb** 51	**Te** 52	iodine **I** 53	**Xe** 54
Pt 78	gold **Au** 79	mercury **Hg** 80	**Tl** 81	lead **Pb** 82	**Bi** 83	**Po** 84	**At** 85	**Rn** 86

non-metals

metals

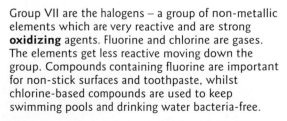

Group VII are the halogens – a group of non-metallic elements which are very reactive and are strong **oxidizing** agents. Fluorine and chlorine are gases. The elements get less reactive moving down the group. Compounds containing fluorine are important for non-stick surfaces and toothpaste, whilst chlorine-based compounds are used to keep swimming pools and drinking water bacteria-free.

Metals and Non-metals

Most of the **elements** in the **Periodic Table** are **metals**, with only 22 of them being **non-metals**. There are fairly clear differences in character between them. Metallic and non-metallic properties can be seen in **compounds** as well as in elements themselves.

Metals

Metals have played an important role in human lives for many thousands of years. Since our distant ancestors first discovered bronze and iron, we have taken advantage of the many useful properties of metals. A few metals, including iron, steel, cobalt, and nickel share a special characteristic— **magnetism**. They are all attracted by magnets and can become magnets themselves under the right circumstances.

The properties of metals have been available for people to use for thousands of years. Here are some of the uses of metal.

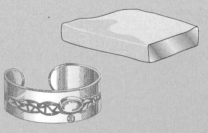

Most metals are shiny solids at room temperature, although in many cases the shine is only apparent when the metal is freshly cut because it reacts with the oxygen in the air to form a dull oxide film.

Metals are good conductors of heat. This is why many cooking pans and cake tins are made of metal. The metal conducts the heat from the heat source to the food that needs to be cooked.

Metals are good conductors of electricity. They allow an electric current to flow through them.

Another reason we use metals so much is because they are relatively easy to shape into whatever we want. They can be hammered or beaten into sheets, pressed into shape, drawn out into wires, melted, and molded.

Non-metals

Non-metals do not share physical characteristics in the way metals do. The appearance of non-metals ranges from colorless **gases** to colored gases, from **liquids** to shiny solids, from dull solids to colored solids, and so on. What they do have in common is that they do not look like metals! Another thing they have in common is that they are almost all poor conductors of heat and electricity. Graphite, one of the forms of carbon, is a notable exception—it can conduct electricity.

Nature's insulators

Non-metals, like the gases of the air, are very poor conductors of heat. For millions of years animals have made use of this fact to help survive extreme temperatures. In cold weather, tiny muscles in the skin of birds and mammals pull their feathers or hair upright to trap a layer of air around the body. This acts as an insulating layer, preventing body heat being lost to the cold surroundings. Humans try the same trick, but we just get goosebumps. Instead, we use clothes to trap layers of air and keep us warm.

▶ Strangely enough, a camel's thick fur helps prevent it from getting too hot during the day! The insulating layer of trapped air prevents the external heat transferring to the body of the camel. The same layer then prevents heat loss from the body during cold nights in the desert.

Glossary

absolute zero   the lowest possible temperature where all **particle** movement stops (0°K, –459°F, –273°C)

atom   the smallest particle of an **element**

atomic number   the number of **protons** in the **nucleus** of an **atom**

boil   to change state from a **liquid** to a **gas**

chemical reaction   when two **elements** or **compounds** react together chemically

chromatography   a way of separating a **mixture** of colored substances

compound   a substance made of two or more different types of **atom** chemically joined together

condense   to change state from a **gas** to a **liquid**

conductor   a substance through which an electric current and/or heat can pass

contract   get smaller

decompression   divers returning to the surface spend hours at different levels to allow the **gases** to **diffuse** slowly out of their blood

diffusion   the mixing or spreading of substances in a **gas** or a **liquid** as a result of the random movement and collisions of the **particles** around them

dissolve   when the **particles** of a **solid** mix with those of a **liquid** so it disappears into the liquid

distillation   separating substances by boiling and allowing one substance to **condense** and be collected

DNA   deoxyribose nucleic acid, the material of genetic inheritance

elastic forces   forces holding **particles** together in a **solid** or **liquid**

electrons   negative **particles** that travel rapidly around the **nucleus** of an **atom**

element   a substance made of only one type of **atom**. There are 91 naturally occurring elements

expand   get bigger

filtration/filter   separating a **solid** from a **liquid** by filtering

fractional distillation   separating a mixture of **liquids** by distilling each one at a different temperature

gas   a state of matter when a substance has no fixed shape or volume

gas pressure   a measure of the number and frequency of the collisions of **gas** particles with the walls of the vessel they are in

genetic fingerprinting   a special technique that makes it possible to separate and identify the **DNA** from any individual person

insoluble   a **solid** that will not **dissolve** in a particular **solvent**

insulator   a poor **conductor** of heat or electricity

isotopes   atoms of the same **element** with the same number of **protons** but different numbers of **neutrons**

K   Kelvin, a measure of temperature

liquid   a state of matter when a substance has a fixed volume but no fixed shape

magnetism   the ability to be attracted by magnets and to become magnetized

mass   how much matter something is made of

melt   to change state from a **solid** to a **liquid**

metal   shiny materials that are good **conductors** of heat and electricity and can be shaped in many ways

mixture   elements or **compounds** that are mixed together physically but do not join chemically

model   a way of trying to explain the way things work

molecule   a **particle** made up of more than one **atom** joined together

methylated spirits   a **solvent** based on ethanol with methanol added to make it poisonous and undrinkable

neutrons   neutral **particles** in the **nucleus** of an **atom**

non-metals   materials that are poor **conductors** of heat and electricity

non-reactive   does not react easily with other chemicals

nucleus   the central part of an **atom** that always contains **protons**

oxidizing   reacting with oxygen to form an oxide

particles   small units of matter, often **atoms** or **molecules**

Periodic Table   a table showing all the **elements** arranged in groups in order of **atomic number**

periods   groups across the **Periodic Table**

physical changes   when a substance changes state but remains chemically the same

plasma   the fourth state of matter found only in stars in space

protons   positive **particles** found in the **nucleus** of an **atom**

radioactive   atoms decay, releasing ionising radiation and forming different **isotopes**

reactant   a chemical taking part in a **chemical reaction**

reactive   reacts very easily with other chemicals

saturated solution   a **solution** in which no more **solid** will **dissolve**

saturation diving   divers working at great depths and living in special chambers that reproduce the same pressure so they do not need repeated **decompression**

solid   a state of matter when a substance has a fixed shape and a fixed volume

solidifies   to change state from a **liquid** to a **solid** or a gas to a solid

solute   the **solid** that dissolves in a **solvent** to form a **solution**

solution   the mixture of the **solid** **solute** dissolved in the liquid **solvent**

solvent   a **liquid** in which some **solids** will **dissolve**

sub-atomic   smaller than an **atom**

sublimation   turning straight from a solid to a gas on heating

transition elements   the large block of **metals** between the main groups of the **Periodic Table**

More Books to Read

Darling, David. *From Glasses to Gasses: The Science of Matter.* Morristown, NJ: Silver Burdett. 1992

Friedhoffer, Robert. *Matter & Energy.* Danbury, CT: Franklin Watts Inc. 1992.

Kerrod, Robin. *Matter & Materials.* Tarrytown, NY: Marshall Cavendish. 1995.

Index